P9-DHF-701

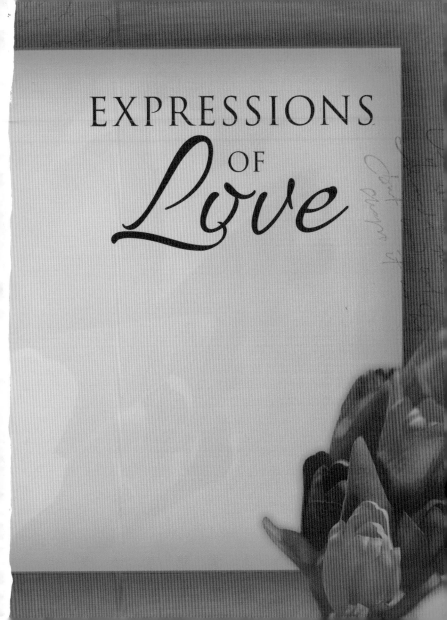

EXPRESSIONS
OF
Love

EXPRESSIONS

OF

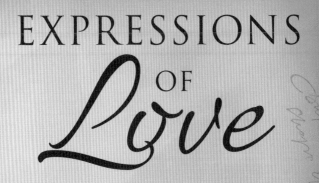

Love

Helen Steiner Rice

BARBOUR
PUBLISHING

© 2007 the Helen Steiner Rice Foundation

ISBN 978-1-59789-825-6

Devotional writing by Rebecca Currington in association with Snapdragon Group ℠ Editorial Services.

The poetry of Helen Steiner Rice is published under a licensing agreement with the Helen Steiner Rice Foundation.

Special thanks to Virginia Ruehlmann for her cooperation and assistance in the development of this book.

Published by Barbour Publishing, Inc., P.O. Box 719, Uhrichsville, Ohio 44683.

Our mission is to publish and distribute inspirational products offering exceptional value and biblical encouragement to the masses.

ecpa Member of the
Evangelical Christian
Publishers Association

Printed in Malaysia.

Contents

God's Love

"Though the mountains be shaken and the hills be removed, yet my unfailing love for you will not be shaken nor my covenant of peace be removed," says the Lord, *who has compassion on you.*

Isaiah 54:10

God loves you, dear friend—constantly, completely, irrevocably. He loves you in spite of your past, in light of your future, and without regard for your social or economic status. God's love is free to all who choose to reach out and take it. Have you opened your heart to the Lover of your soul? Have you felt the glory of being immersed in His love? We do not know why He chooses to love us—only that He does. Praise His name!

7

No matter what your past has been,

Trust God to understand.

And no matter what your problem is

Just place it in His hand—

For in all of our unloveliness

This great God loves us still.

He loved us since the world began

And what's more, He always will.

God's love is like an island

in life's ocean vast and wide—

A peaceful, quiet shelter

from the restless, rising tide. . .

God's love is like a fortress,

and we seek protection there

When the waves of tribulation

seem to drown us in despair. . .

God's love is like a beacon

burning bright with faith and prayer,

And through the changing scenes of life,

we can find a haven there!

*W*hat more can we ask of our Father

Than to know we are never alone,

That His mercy and love are unfailing,

And He makes all our problems His own.

We are all God's children

    and He loves us, every one.

He freely and completely forgives

    all that we have done,

Asking only if we're ready

    to follow where He leads,

Content that in His wisdom

    He will answer all our needs.

If we confess our sins, he is faithful and just and will forgive us our sins and purify us from all unrighteousness.

1 JOHN 1:9

What is love? No words can define it—

It's something so great

    only God could design it.

For love means much more

    than small words can express

For what we call love is very much less

Than the beauty and depth

    and the true richness of

God's gift to mankind—

    His compassionate love.

Somebody loves you more than you know,

Somebody goes with you wherever you go,

Somebody really and truly cares

And lovingly listens to all of your prayers.

And if you walk in His footsteps

and have faith to believe,

There's nothing you ask for

that you will not receive.

Kings and kingdoms all pass away—

Nothing on earth endures. . .

But the love of God who sent His Son

Is forever and ever yours!

Wait with a heart that is patient

For the goodness of God to prevail—

For never do prayers go unanswered,

And His mercy and love never fail.

God's love is like a sanctuary where our

souls can find sweet rest

From the struggle and the tension of

life's fast and futile quest.

"Come to me, all you who are weary and burdened, and I will give you rest."

MATTHEW 11:28

The sky and the stars, the waves and the sea,
The dew on the grass, the leaves on the tree
Are constant reminders of
    God and His nearness,
Proclaiming His presence
    with crystal-like clearness.
So how could I think God was far, far away
When I feel Him beside me
    every hour of the day?
And I've plenty of reasons
    to know God's my friend
And this is one friendship
    that time cannot end!

Don't doubt for a minute

that this is not true,

For God loves His children

and takes care of them, too. . .

And all of His treasures

are yours to share

If you love Him completely

and show that you care. . .

And if you walk in His footsteps

and have faith to believe,

There's nothing you ask for

that you will not receive.

Friendship

Two people are better off than one, for they can help each other succeed. If one person falls, the other can reach out and help.

ECCLESIASTES 4:9–10 NLT

The world we live in can be harsh and unwelcoming, intolerant of our mistakes. God knew we would need friends to encourage us along the way. He knew we would need others to laugh with, sing with, dream with. He knew we would need comfort and support and loving-kindness. Cherish your friends; hold them close. They are very special people, for they do God's work in your life.

Friendship is a priceless gift
That can't be bought or sold,
But to have an understanding
    friend
Is worth far more than gold.

Across the years we've met in dreams

And shared each other's hopes and schemes,

We knew a friendship rich and rare

And beauty far beyond compare.

Then you reached out your arms for more,

To catch what you were yearning for.

But little did you think or guess

That one can't capture happiness

Because it's unrestrained and free,

Unfettered by reality.

We lock up our hearts and fail to heed

The outstretched hand, reaching to find

A kindred spirit whose heart and mind

Are lonely and longing to somehow share

Our joys and sorrows

    and to make us aware

That life's completeness

    and richness depends

On the things we share

    with our loved ones and friends.

Thank you for your friendship

And your understanding of

The folks who truly love you

And the folks you truly love.

"Love one another. As I have loved
you, so you must love one another. By
this all men will know that you are my
disciples, if you love one another."

JOHN 13:34–35

Friends and prayers are priceless treasures

Beyond all monetary measures,

And so I say a special prayer

That God will keep you in His care.

For the friends that we make

are life's gift of love,

And I think friends are sent

right from heaven above.

And thinking of you

somehow makes me feel

That God is love and He's very real.

Among the great and glorious gifts

    our heavenly Father sends

Is the gift of understanding

    that we find in loving friends,

For it's not money or gifts

    or material things,

But understanding the joy it brings,

That can change this old world

    in wonderful ways

And put goodness and mercy

    back in our days.

Friendship, like flowers,

blooms ever more fair

When carefully tended by

dear friends who care;

And life's lovely garden

would be sweeter by far

If all who passed through it

were as nice as you are.

Every day's a good day

    to lose yourself in others

And any time a good time

    to see mankind as brothers,

And this can only happen

    when you realize it's true

That everyone needs someone

    and that someone is you.

If people like me didn't know

people like you,

Life would lose its meaning

and its richness, too.

Gold is cold and lifeless,

    it cannot see nor hear,

And in your times of trouble,

    it is powerless to cheer.

It has no ears to listen,

    no heart to understand.

It cannot bring you comfort

    or reach out a helping hand.

So when you ask God for a gift,

    be thankful that He sends,

Not diamonds, pearls, or riches,

    but the love of a real, true friend.

*Dear children, let us not love with words
or tongue but with actions and in truth.*

1 JOHN 3:18

For in this world of trouble

that is filled with anxious care,

Everybody needs a friend

in whom they're free to share

The little secret heartaches

that lay heavy on their mind.

We seek our true and trusted friend

in the knowledge that we'll find

A heart that's sympathetic

and an understanding mind.

Like roses in a garden, kindness fills the air

With a certain bit of sweetness

as it touches everywhere.

For kindness is a circle that never, never ends

But just keeps ever-widening

in the circle of our friends.

For the more you give, the more you get

is proven every day,

And so to get the most from life

you must give yourself away.

You're like a ray of sunshine

Or a star up in the sky,

You add a special brightness

Whenever you pass by.

For in this raucous, restless world

We're small, but God is great,

And in His love, dear friend,

Our hearts communicate!

*F*ather, make us kind and wise

So we may always recognize

The blessings that are ours to take,

The friendships that are ours to make,

If we but open our heart's door wide

To let the sunshine of love inside.

Like ships upon the sea of life

    we meet with friends so dear,

Then sail on swiftly from the ones

    we'd like to linger near;

Sometimes I wish the winds would cease,

    the waves be quiet, too,

And let me sort of drift along

    beside a friend like you.

Nothing on earth can make

life more worthwhile

Than a true, loyal friend

and the warmth of a smile,

For, just like a sunbeam makes

the cloudy days brighter,

The smile of a friend makes

a heavy heart lighter.

Family

Love must be sincere. Hate what is evil; cling to what is good. Be devoted to one another in brotherly love. Honor one another above yourselves.

ROMANS 12:9–10

What is deeper, more constant than a mother's love and a father's love? It is the truest affection we can know. That's how God loves each of us. To prove it, He has placed us in families, where such love can be expressed in human terms—hugs, kisses, verbal assurances, and encouragement. Family is God's gift to us. Thank Him for each member of your biological family, your family of friends, and your spiritual family made up of fellow believers.

LOVE IS THE LANGUAGE
    THAT EVERY HEART SPEAKS,
FOR LOVE IS ONE THING
    THAT EVERY HEART SEEKS. . .
AND WHERE THERE IS LOVE
    GOD, TOO, WILL ABIDE
AND BLESS THE FAMILY
    RESIDING INSIDE.

There's a road I call remembrance

    where I walk each day with you.

It's a pleasant, happy road, my dear,

    all filled with memories true.

Today it leads me through a spot

    where I can dream awhile,

And in its tranquil peacefulness

    I touch your hand and smile.

It takes a mother's kindness

  to forgive us when we err,

To sympathize in trouble

  and bow her head in prayer.

It takes a mother's wisdom

  to recognize our needs

And to give us reassurance

  by her loving words and deeds.

Tender little memories

of some word or deed

Give us strength and courage

when we are in need.

Blessed little memories

help to bear the cross

And soften all the bitterness

of failure and of loss.

Precious little memories

of little things we've done

Make the very darkest day

a bright and happy one.

The LORD reigns, let the earth be glad;
let the distant shores rejoice.

$\mathscr{M}$ emories to treasure

are made every day—

Made of family gatherings

and children as they play.

A mother's love is something

    that no one can explain—

It is made of deep devotion

    and sacrifice and pain.

It believes beyond believing

    when the world around condemns,

And it glows with all the beauty

    of the rarest, brightest gems.

A many-splendored miracle

    we cannot understand

And another wondrous evidence of

    God's tender, guiding hand.

Across the years we've met in dreams

And shared each other's hopes and schemes,

We knew a friendship rich and rare

And beauty far beyond compare.

A mother's love is like an island

In life's ocean vast and wide—

A peaceful, quiet shelter

From the restless, rising tide.

A mother's love is like a beacon

Burning bright with faith and prayer,

And through the changing scenes of life,

We can find a haven there.

For a mother's love is fashioned

After God's enduring love—

It is endless and unfailing

Like the love of Him above.

55

IN SEEKING PEACE FOR ALL PEOPLE

THERE IS ONLY ONE PLACE TO BEGIN

AND THAT IS IN EACH HOME AND HEART—

FOR THE FORTRESS OF PEACE IS WITHIN.

In my eyes there lies no vision

    but the sight of your dear face.

In my heart there is no feeling

    but the warmth of your embrace.

In my mind there are no thoughts

    but the thoughts of you, my dear.

In my soul no other longing

    but just to have you near.

All my dreams were built around you,

    and I've come to know it's true,

In my life there is no living

    that is not a part of you.

And where the home is filled with love

You'll always find God spoken of,

And when a family prays together

That family also stays together.

Ascribe to the LORD the glory due his name; worship the LORD in the splendor of his holiness.

PSALM 29:2

It is sharing and caring,
Giving and forgiving,
Loving and being loved,
Walking hand in hand,
Talking heart to heart,
Seeing through each other's eyes,
Laughing together,
Weeping together,
Praying together,
And always trusting and believing
And thanking God for each other. . .
For love that is shared is a beautiful thing—
It enriches the soul and makes the heart sing.

There are hills and fields and budding trees

and stillness that's so sweet.

That it seems that this must be the place

where God and humans meet.

I hope we can go back again

and golden hours renew,

And God go with you always, dear,

until the day we do.

Time cannot destroy the memory,

and years can never erase

The tenderness and the beauty

of the love in a mother's face.

And when we think of our mothers,

we draw nearer to God above,

For only God in His greatness

could fashion a mother's love.

A baby is a gift of life

   born of the wonder of love—

A little bit of eternity

   sent from the Father above,

Giving a new dimension to the love

   between husband and wife

And putting an added new meaning

   to the wonder and mystery of life.

A wee bit of heaven drifted

    down from above—

A handful of happiness a heart full of love.

The mystery of life so sacred and sweet,

The giver of joy so deep and complete.

Precious and priceless, so lovable, too—

The world's sweetest miracle, baby, is you.

In any kind of trouble

    Dad reaches out his hand,

And you can always count on him

    to help and understand. . .

And while we do not praise Dad

    as often as we should,

We love him and admire him,

    and while that's understood,

It's only fair to emphasize

    his importance and his worth,

For if there were no loving dads,

    this would be a loveless earth.

Love's Power

We are more than conquerors through him who loved us. For I am convinced that neither death nor life, neither angels nor demons, neither the present nor the future, nor any powers, neither height nor depth, nor anything else in all creation, will be able to separate us from the love of God that is in Christ Jesus our Lord.

ROMANS 8:37–39

God's love is powerful enough to save us from ourselves and transform our lives. It can reach to any height or depth. It has no limitations. When we love others, we are like Him—powerful! We can encourage the weary soul, comfort the bereaved, revive the downhearted. We can change lives and inspire eternal results. God's power is in His love, His power to heal and restore. Receive His love, and pass it on to others.

Great is the power of might and mind,

But only love can make us kind.

And all we are or hope to be

Is empty pride and vanity.

If love is not a part of all,

The greatest man is very small.

There are no safety boxes or vaults
    that cannot contain
The possessions we collected
    and desire to retain. . .
So all that man acquires, be it power,
    fame, or jewels,
Is but limited and earthly,
    only treasure made for fools. . .
For only in God's kingdom can man find
    enduring treasure,
Priceless gifts of love and beauty—
    more than mortal man can measure,
And the riches he accumulates
    he can keep and part with never,
For only in God's kingdom
    do our treasures last forever. . .
So use the word *forever* with sanctity and love,
For nothing is forever
    but the love of God above!

To be in God's keeping is surely a blessing,

For though life is often dark and distressing,

No day is too dark and no burden too great

That God in His love cannot penetrate.

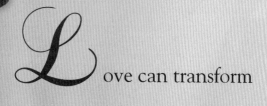

$\mathcal{L}$ove can transform

the most commonplace

Into beauty and kindness

and goodness and grace.

But the fruit of the Spirit is love,
joy, peace, patience, kindness,
goodness, faithfulness, gentleness
and self-control. Against such
things there is no law.

GALATIANS 5:22–23

The flower of love and devotion has

guided me all through my life;

Softening my grief and my trouble,

sharing my toil and strife.

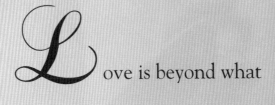

Love is beyond what

man can define

For love is immortal

and God's gift is divine.

Love's too great to understand,

But just to clasp a loved one's hand

Can change the darkness into light

And make the heart take wingless flight.

With love in our hearts, let us try this year

To lift the clouds of hate and fear,

For love works in ways

    that are wondrous and strange,

And there is nothing in life

    that love cannot change.

The great and small. . .the good and bad,

The young and old. . .the sad and glad

Are asking today, "Is life worth living?"

And the answer is only

in loving and giving—

For only love can make mankind,

And kindness of heart

brings peace of mind.

Man is powerless alone

    to clean up the world outside

Until his own polluted soul

    is clean and free inside. . .

For the amazing power of love

    is beyond all comprehension

And it alone can heal this world

    of its hatred and dissension.

Love is enduring and patient and kind,

It judges all things with the heart,

   not the mind.

And love can transform

   the most commonplace

Into beauty and splendor

   and sweetness and grace.

"Love one another. As I have loved you, so you must love one another."

JOHN 13:34

Love works in ways

    that are wondrous and strange,

And there is nothing in life

    that cannot change;

And all that God promised

    will someday come true

When you have loved one another

    the way He loved you.

Love is unselfish, understanding, and kind,

For it sees with its heart and

not with its mind.

Love is the answer that

everyone seeks—

Love is the language that

every heart speaks—

Love can't be bought,

it is priceless and free,

Love like pure magic

is a sweet mystery.

Love's Comfort

There is no fear in love.
But perfect love drives out fear.

1 JOHN 4:18

You may be at a low point in your life, dear friend. You may have suffered tragedy or disappointment or discouragement. You are not alone. God is at your side. If you will let Him, He is eager to help carry your burden. He longs to comfort you and remind you of the blessings in your life. Open your heart to Him. Invite Him to help you with your trouble. He will not disappoint you.

I said a little prayer for you,

and I asked the Lord above

To keep you safely in His care

and enfold you in His love.

I did not ask for fortune,

for riches, or for fame,

I only asked for blessings

in the Savior's Holy name.

Blessings to surround you

in times of trial and stress,

And inner joy to fill your heart

with peace and happiness.

God in His goodness has promised

that the cross He gives us to wear

Will never exceed our endurance or be

more than our strength can bear. . .

And secure in that blessed assurance,

we can smile as we face tomorrow,

For God holds the key to the future,

and no sorrow or care need we borrow.

The earth is the Lord's

    and the fullness thereof,

It speaks of His greatness

    and it sings of His love.

It whispers of mysteries

    we cannot comprehend,

Of a beautiful land

    where life has no end.

Thank You, God, for the beauty

around me everywhere:

The gentle rain and glistening dew,

the sunshine and the air,

The joyous gift of feeling

the soul's soft, whispering voice,

That speaks to me from deep within

and makes my heart rejoice.

"Always giving thanks to God the Father for everything, in the name of our Lord Jesus Christ."

EPHESIANS 5:20

I am the Way, so just follow Me

Though the way be rough

    and you cannot see.

I am the Truth, which all men seek,

So heed not false prophets

    or the words that they speak.

I am the Life and I hold the key

That opens the door to eternity.

And in this dark world, I am the Light

To a Promised Land

    where there is no night.

His love knows no exceptions

    so never feel excluded;

No matter who or what you are,

    your name has been included—

And no matter what your past has been,

    trust God to understand,

And no matter what your problem is

    just place it in His hand.

I know He stilled the tempest

and calmed the angry sea,

And I humbly ask if in His love

He'll do the same for me.

God, be my resting place
and my protection
In hours of trouble, defeat,
and dejection.
May I never give way
to self-pity and sorrow,
May I always be sure
of a better tomorrow.
May I stand undaunted, come what may,
Secure in the knowledge
I have only to pray
And ask my Creator and Father above
To keep me serene in His grace
and His love.

The love of God surrounds us

Like the air we breathe around us—

As near as a heartbeat,

as close as a prayer,

And whenever we need Him,

He'll always be there.

"And surely I am with you always,
to the very end of the age."

The rainbow is God's promise

Of hope for you and me,

And though the clouds hang heavy

And the sun we cannot see,

We know above the dark clouds

That fill the stormy sky,

Hope's rainbow will come shining through

When the clouds have drifted by.

Someone cares and always will,

The world forgets but God loves you still,

You cannot go beyond His love

No matter what you're guilty of—

Someone cares and loves you still

And God is the someone who always will.

Love's Pricelessness

How priceless is your unfailing love! Both high and low among men find refuge in the shadow of your wings.

PSALM 36:7

How can the price of God's love be measured? He loved us enough to create us. He loved us enough to give us a free will. He loved us enough to pay the highest imaginable price to buy us back when we chose poorly and gave ourselves to another. Even now, He loves us more than we can know. He lovingly hears our prayers and guides our steps. God's love is not free, but it will cost you nothing, dear friend. Reach out to Him, and you will receive.

Love is like a priceless treasure

which there is no way to measure.

For who can fathom stars or sea

or figure the length of eternity?

And blessed are they who walk in love,

for love's a gift from God above.

It can't be bought. It can't be sold.

It can't be measured in silver and gold.

It's a special wish that God above

Will fill your heart with peace and love—

The love of God, which is divine,

That is beyond what words can define,

So you may know the comfort of

God's all-fulfilling grace and love.

Love means much more

　　than small words can express,

For what we call love

　　is so very much less

Than the beauty and depth

　　and the true richness of

God's gift to mankind—

　　His compassionate love.

The priceless gift of life is love.

For with the help of God above,

Love dissolves all hate and fear

And makes our vision bright and clear,

So we can see and rise above

Our pettiness on wings of love.

A man's wisdom gives him patience;
it is to his glory to overlook an offense.

PROVERBS 19:11

$\mathcal{L}$ove is a gift to treasure forever

Given by God without price tag or measure. . .

Love is a gift we all can possess,

Love is a key to the soul's happiness.

Love is much more than a tender caress
And more than bright hours
  of happiness,
For a lasting love is made up of sharing
Both hours that are joyous
  and also despairing.
It's made up of patience
  and deep understanding
And never of stubborn
  or selfish demanding.
It's made up of climbing
  the steep hills together
And facing with courage
  life's stormiest weather.

LOVE IS UNSELFISH,

UNDERSTANDING, AND KIND,

FOR IT SEES WITH ITS HEART

AND NOT WITH ITS MIND.

Love can't be bought—

  it is priceless and free.

Love, like pure magic,

  is a sweet mystery.

$\mathcal{L}$ove is the answer that

everyone seeks.

Love is the language

that every heart speaks.

Love covers over all wrongs.

PROVERBS 10:12

With our hands we give gifts

    that money can buy—

Diamonds that sparkle

    like stars in the sky,

Trinkets that glitter

    like the sun as it rises,

Beautiful baubles

    that come as surprises—

But only our hearts can feel real love

And share the gift of our Father above.

What is love? No words can define it—

It's something so great

    only God could design it.

Wonder of wonders,

    beyond our conception,

And only in God

    can love find true perfection.

Loving Others

We know what real love is because Jesus
gave up his life for us. So we also ought to
give up our lives for our brothers and sisters.

1 JOHN 3:16 NLT

God's love, dear friend, cannot be
contained. It fills the willing heart to
overflowing and the result is that we
love others as He has loved us. Every
kindness, every tenderness, every word of
encouragement, every smile, every loving
act springs from the divine fountain that
gushes forth from our souls. Have you
received God's love? Then you need only
do what comes naturally—allow His love
to flow to others.

For every day's a good day

    to lose yourself in others

And any time a good time

    to see mankind as brothers,

And this can only happen

    when you realize it's true

That everyone needs someone

    and that someone is you!

Kindness is a virtue given by the Lord,

It pays dividends in happiness

and joy is its reward. . .

For if you practice kindness

in all you say and do,

The Lord will wrap His kindness

around your heart and you.

Every day is a reason for giving,

And giving is the key to living.

So let us give ourselves away,

Not just today but every day.

When you do what you do

    with a will and a smile. . .

Everything that you do

    will seem twice as worthwhile. . .

When you walk down the street,

    life will seem twice as sweet

If you smile at the people

    you happen to meet. . .

For when you smile, it is true,

    folks will smile back at you.

Rejoice in the Lord always.
I will say it again: Rejoice!

PHILIPPIANS 4:4

A kind and thoughtful deed

Or a hand outstretched in a time of need

Is the rarest of gifts, for it is a part,

Not of the purse but a loving heart.

The more you give, the more you get—

The more you laugh, the less you fret—

The more you do unselfishly,

The more you live abundantly.

The more of everything you share,

The more you'll always have to spare—

The more you love, the more you'll find

That life is good and friends are kind. . .

For only what we give away,

enriches us from day to day.

No one is a stranger in God's sight,

For God is love and in His light

May we, too, try in our small way

To make new friends from day to day. . .

So pass no stranger with an unseeing eye,

For God may be sending a new friend by.

To love one another as God loved you

May seem impossible to do,

But if you will try to have faith and believe

There's no end to the joy that you will receive.

Therefore, as God's chosen people,
holy and dearly loved, clothe
yourselves with compassion, kindness,
humility, gentleness and patience.

COLOSSIANS 3:12

Love is the answer to all the heart seeks,

And love is the channel

    through which God speaks—

And all He has promised can only come true

When you love one another

    the way He loved you.

Great is our gladness

    to serve God through others,

For our Father taught us

    we all are sisters and brothers,

And the people we meet

    on life's thoroughfares

Are burdened with trouble

    and sorrow and cares,

And this is the chance

    we are given each day

To witness for God

    to learn and obey.

A cheerful smile, a friendly word,

  a sympathetic nod,

All priceless little treasures

  from the storehouse of our God—

They are the things that can't be bought

  with silver or with gold,

For thoughtfulness and kindness

  and love are never sold—

They are the priceless things in life

  for which no one can pay,

And the giver finds rich recompense

  in giving them away.

Only what we give away

Enriches us from day to day,

For not in getting but in giving

Is found the lasting joy of living,

For no one ever had a part

In sharing treasures of the heart

Who did not feel the impact of

The magic mystery of God's love.

Love alone can make us kind

And give us joy and peace of mind,

So live with joy unselfishly

And you'll be blessed abundantly.

Romance, Commitment, and Marriage

Most important of all, continue to show deep love for each other, for love covers a multitude of sins.

I PETER 4:8 NLT

Marriage is a sturdy structure, designed to provide love and intimacy and companionship throughout our lives. It is more than romance. It is romance plus commitment—so that we don't lose our bearings when the feelings ebb and flow. Rejoice in the one God has given you, dear friend. Being true to your spouse is being true to God. He will be pleased by your faithfulness and love.

You cannot go beyond my thoughts

or leave my love behind,

Because I keep you in my heart

and forever in my mind.

And though I may not tell you,

I think you know it's true

That I find daily happiness

in the very thought of you.

Old nighttime brings me nearer

To the one I love so well,

And twinkling stars and moonbeams

Ne'er get a chance to tell.

And although we are far apart,

Your face I almost see,

For stars that take your message

Are smiling back at me.

There is comfort just in longing

For a smile from your dear face,

And joy in just remembering

Each sweet and fond embrace.

There is happiness in knowing

That my heart will always be

A place where I can hold you

And keep you near to me.

Love is a many-splendored thing,

The greatest joy that life can bring,

And let no one try to disparage

The sacred bond of holy marriage,

For love is not love until God above

Sanctifies the union of two people in love.

Marriage should be honored by all.

Hebrews 13:4

What is marriage?
It is sharing and caring,
Giving and forgiving,
Loving and being loved,
Walking hand in hand,
Talking heart to heart,
Seeing through each other's eyes,
Laughing together,
Weeping together,
Praying together,
And always trusting and believing
And thanking God for each other.
For love that is shared
    is a beautiful thing;
It enriches the soul and
makes the heart sing.

In my eyes there lies no vision

    but the sight of your dear face,

In my heart there is no feeling

    but the warmth of your embrace.

In my mind there are no thoughts

    thoughts of you, my dear,

In my soul, no other longing

    but just to have you near.

All my dreams are built around you,

    and I've come to know it's true—

In my life there is no living

    that is not a part of you.

Happy little memories

    go flitting through my mind,

And in all my thoughts and memories

    I always seem to find

The picture of your face, dear,

    the memory of your touch

And all the other little things

    I've come to love so much.

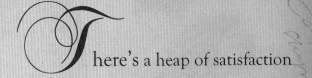

here's a heap of satisfaction

to sit here thinking of you

And to tell you once again, dear,

how very much I love you.

Dear God,

Please help me in my feeble way

To somehow do something each day

To show the one I love the best

My faith in him will stand each test.

And let me show in some small way

The love I have for him each day

And prove beyond all doubt and fear

That his love for me I hold most dear.

And so I ask of God above—

Just make me worthy of his love.

Submit to one another out of reverence for Christ.

EPHESIANS 5:21

There are things we cannot measure,

    like the depths of waves and sea

And the heights of stars in heaven

    and the joy you bring to me.

Like eternity's long endlessness

    and the sunset's golden hue,

There is no way to measure

    the love I have for you.

You put the love in loveliness

And the sweet in sweetness, too.

I think they took life's dearest things

And wrapped them up in you.

So keep me in your heart, dear,

And in your every prayer,

For wherever you are, darling,

I like to feel I'm there.

Love is much more than a tender caress

And more than bright hours

   of happiness,

For a lasting love is made up of sharing

Both hours that are joyous

   and also despairing.

It's made up of patience

   and deep understanding.

You're lovable; you're wonderful;

You're as sweet as you can be.

There's no one in all the world

Who means so much to me;

I love you more than life itself,

You make my dreams come true,

Forever is not long enough

For me to be near you.

Healing Love

Confess your sins to each other and pray for each other so that you may be healed. The earnest prayer of a righteous person has great power and produces wonderful results.

JAMES 5:16 NLT

The love of God does many things in our lives—but most of all, it heals us. It transforms our broken lives and squandered possibilities into tapestries of great beauty. It makes all things new. No matter how old you are, how much water has passed under the bridge in your life, how many mistakes you've made, with God you have the chance to begin tomorrow with hope, dear friend. He is the God who heals you.

Where there is love the heart is light,

Where there is love the day is bright,

Where there is love there is quiet peace,

A tranquil place where turmoils cease.

Oh, God, what a comfort to know

that you care

And to know when I seek You,

You will always be there.

MAY HE WHO LIVED IN GALILEE

AND HEALED THE MANY THERE

BE NEAR TO YOU AND HEAL YOU, TOO,

AND KEEP YOU IN HIS CARE.

It's not money or gifts or material things,

But understanding and the joy it brings,

That can change this old world
   in wonderful ways

And put goodness and mercy
   back in our days.

"A man's life does not consist in the abundance of his possessions."

LUKE 12:15

Oh, Blessed Father, hear this prayer,

And keep all of us in Your care,

Give us patience and inner sight, too,

Just as You often used to do

When on the shores of the Galilee

You touched the blind and they could see

And cured the man who long was lame

When he but called Your holy name.

While life's a mystery we can't understand

The great Giver of life is holding our hand,

And safe in His care

    there is no need for seeing,

For in Him we live and move

    and have our being.

All around on every side,

    new life and joy appear

To tell us nothing ever dies

    and we should have no fear,

For death is just a detour

    along life's winding way

That leads God's chosen children

    to a bright and glorious day.

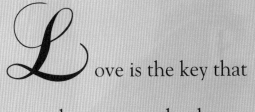

ove is the key that

throws open the door

To the heart that was locked

and lonely before.

Keep on believing, whatever betide you,

Knowing that God will be

    with you to guide you. . .

And all that He promised

    will be yours to receive

If you trust Him completely

    and always believe.

"If you believe, you will receive whatever you ask for in prayer."

MATTHEW 21:22

When you're troubled and worried

  and sick at heart

And your plans are upset

  and your world falls apart,

Remember God's ready

  and waiting to share

The burden you find too heavy to bear.

So with faith, let go

  and let God lead the way

Into a brighter and less troubled day.

In sickness or health,

In suffering and pain,

In storm-laden skies,

In sunshine and rain,

God always is there

To lighten your way

And lead you through darkness

To a much brighter day.

The house of prayer is no farther away

Than the quiet spot

   where you kneel and pray,

For the heart is a temple

   when God is there

As you place yourself in His loving care.

God can remove our uncertain fear

And replace our worry

    with healing cheer. . .

So close your eyes and open your heart

And let God come in and freely impart

A brighter outlook

    and new courage, too,

As His spiritual sunshine

    smiles on you.

Eternal Love

*Three things will last forever—faith, hope,
and love—and the greatest of these is love.*

1 CORINTHIANS 13:13 NLT

Even the most exquisite forms of human love are fallible. But God's love never fails. It does not change with circumstances or seek revenge when it is rebuffed. God's love is pure—and it's eternal. It provides shelter from the storms of life and more joy than the human heart can contain. It is the basis for which all love exists. Submit your lonely heart to Him, dear friend. Experience His eternal love.

Nothing on earth or in heaven can part

A love that has grown

   to be part of the heart;

And just like the sun

   and the stars and sea,

This love will go on through eternity.

For true love lives on

   when earthly things die,

For it's part of the spirit

   that soars in the sky.

It's amazing and incredible,

but it's as true as it can be—

God loves and understands us all,

and that means you and me.

God's kindness is ever around you,

always ready to freely impart

Strength to your faltering spirit,

cheer to your lonely heart.

So how could I think God

was far, far away

When I feel Him beside me

every hour of the day?

And I've plenty of reasons

to know God's my friend

And this is one friendship

that time cannot end!

Come near to God and
he will come near to you.

JAMES 4:8

[Love is] endless and unselfish and enduring,

come what may,

For nothing can destroy it

or take that love away.

[Love is] patient and forgiving

when all others are forsaking,

And it never fails or falters

even though the heart is breaking.

Nothing on earth or in heaven can part

A love that has grown

to be part of the heart. . .

God's love endureth forever—

what a wonderful thing to know

When the tides of life run against you

and your spirit is downcast and low. . .

[GOD HAS] LOVE THAT IS

BIGGER THAN RACE OR CREED

TO COVER THE WORLD AND

FULFILL EACH NEED.

So wait with a heart that is patient

    for the goodness of God to prevail—

For never do prayers go unanswered,

    and His mercy and love never fail.

Be still before the L<small>ORD</small>
and wait patiently for him.

P<small>SALM</small> 37:7

Knowing God's love is unfailing, and

His mercy unending and great,

You have but to trust in His promise,

"God comes not too soon or too late."

*J*ust like the sun and

the stars and the sea,

True love will go on through

eternity.

I take thee to be my partner for life,

To love and live with as

husband and wife;

To have and to hold forever, sweetheart,

Through sickness and health

until death do us part.

Through long, happy years

of caring and sharing,

Secure in the knowledge

that we are preparing

A love that is endless and never can die

But finds its fulfillment

with You in the sky.

Let me serve You every day

And feel You near me when I pray.

Oh, hear my prayer, dear God above,

And make me worthy of Your love.

"Through Jesus, therefore, let us
continually offer to God a sacrifice of
praise—the fruit of lips that confess
his name."

HEBREWS 13:15

189

*For God so loved the world that
he gave his one and only Son, that
whoever believes in him shall not
perish but have eternal life.*

JOHN 3:16

America's beloved inspirational poet laureate, **Helen Steiner Rice**, has encouraged millions of people through her beautiful and uplifting verse. Born in Lorain, Ohio, in 1900, Helen was the daughter of a railroad man and an accomplished seamstress and began writing poetry at a young age.

In 1918, Helen began working for a public utilities company and eventually became one of the first female advertising managers and public speakers in the country. In January 1929, she married a wealthy banker named Franklin Rice, who later sank into depression during the Great Depression and eventually committed suicide. Helen later said that her suffering made her sensitive to the pain of others. Her sadness helped her to write some of her most uplifting verses.

Her work for a Cincinnati, Ohio, greeting card company eventually led to her nationwide popularity as a poet when her Christmas card poem "The Priceless Gift of Christmas," was first read on the Lawrence Welk Show. Soon Helen had produced several books of her poetry that were a source of inspiration to millions of readers.

Helen died in 1981, leaving a foundation in her name to offer assistance to the needy and the elderly. Now more than twenty-five years after her death, Helen's words still speak powerfully to the hearts of readers about love and comfort, faith and hope, peace and joy.